Q&A Kids

FOOD CHAINS

AMY CHAPMAN ANGELIKA SCUDAMORE

WINDMILL BOOKS

Published in 2026 by Windmill Books,
an Imprint of Rosen Publishing
2544 Clinton St.
Buffalo, NY 14224

First published in Great Britain in 2026
by Wayland

Editor: Sarah Peutrill
Designer: Lisa Peacock

Some of the text in this book was first
published in Fact Cat: Food Chains by
Izzi Howell

Cataloging-in-Publication Data

Names: Chapman, Amy, author. | Scudamore, Angelika, illustrator.
Title: Food chains / Amy Chapman, illustrated by Angelika Scudamore.
Description: Buffalo, NY : Windmill Books, 2026. | Series: Q & A kids | Includes glossary and index.
Identifiers: ISBN 9781725396166 (pbk.) | ISBN 9781725396173 (library bound) | ISBN 9781725396180 (ebook)
Subjects: LCSH: Food chains (Ecology)--Juvenile literature.
Classification: LCC QH541.14 C437 2026 | DDC 577'.16--dc23

Printed in the United States of America

CPSIA Compliance Information: Batch #CSWM26
For Further Information contact Rosen Publishing
at 1-800-237-9932

Find us on

CONTENTS

Can you spot the mice in this book? There are 11 to find, not counting me.

LIVING THINGS

Q. Is a food chain a place that sells lots of food everywhere?

A. No! A food chain shows how plants and animals get their energy.

This book explores what food chains are and has lots of examples of different types. But before you learn about them, you need to know a little about living things.

Plants and animals are living things. This means that they grow, change, and, one day, will die. All living things need food and water to survive. Food gives them energy.

FIND IT

In the picture find two types of plant and three types of animal.

PLANTS

Q. What do plants eat?

A. Plants are able to make their own food. They don't have to find food like humans do.

Plants make their own food in their leaves using sunlight, air, and water. There are many different types, or species, of plant. They live in different habitats all over the world.

MATCH IT

Can you match the plants to the habitats they come from?

Water lilies

Desert

Cactus

Pond

Seaweed

Garden

Rose

Ocean

ANIMALS

Q. Can animals make their own food like plants do?

A. No, all animals have to find food to eat to give them energy.

Animals have to eat other living things in order to survive. In every habitat there are different foods for animals to eat.

Bears eat plants and other animals, such as fish.

Toucans eat fruit and also other animals, such as insects.

Rabbits eat plants such as grass.

Giraffes eat the leaves of trees.

Eagles eat small mammals and birds.

Koalas eat leaves from eucalyptus trees.

Lions eat other animals, such as zebras.

HERBIVORES

Q. Do other animals eat the same things we do?

A. No, different animals eat different things.

There are three different types of animal diet: herbivore, carnivore, and omnivore.

Herbivores are animals that eat only plants. Horses and rabbits are examples of herbivores.

COUNT IT

How many rabbits can you spot?

CARNIVORES AND OMNIVORES

Q. Do some animals only eat other animals?

A. Yes, some animals can only eat meat.

Animals that eat other animals for food are called carnivores. Crocodiles and lions are examples of carnivores.

Omnivores, such as bears and blackbirds, eat both plants and animals. Ants are omnivores. They eat other insects and fruit.

SORT IT

Can you sort out the carnivores from the omnivores?

A. Dragonfly

B. Thrush

C. Chicken

D. Tiger

E. Wolf

F. Bear

G. Wasp

H. Hawk

PREDATORS AND PREY

Q. Are predators always carnivores?

A. Predators can be carnivores or omnivores.

Predators are animals that kill other animals for food. Herbivores are usually prey. This means that other animals eat them for food.

Some predators, such as tigers, have big teeth and claws to help them catch prey. To keep safe, some types of prey have good eyesight and hearing so that they can tell when a predator is nearby.

Some carnivores and omnivores eat animals that are already dead. Animals that do this are called scavengers.

MATCH IT

Carnivores have different kinds of teeth than herbivores. Try to match the teeth to the correct animal.

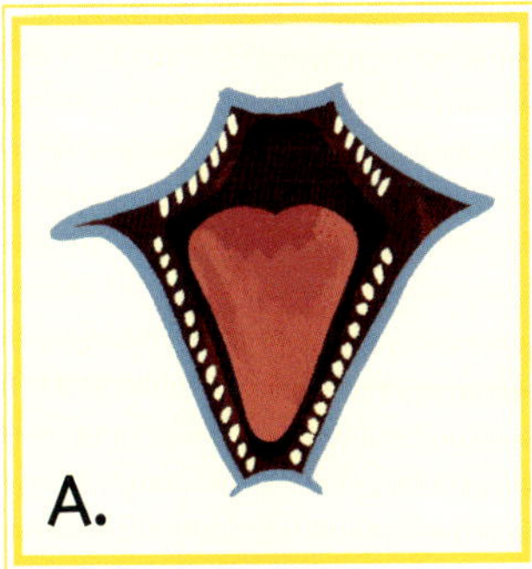

Tiger

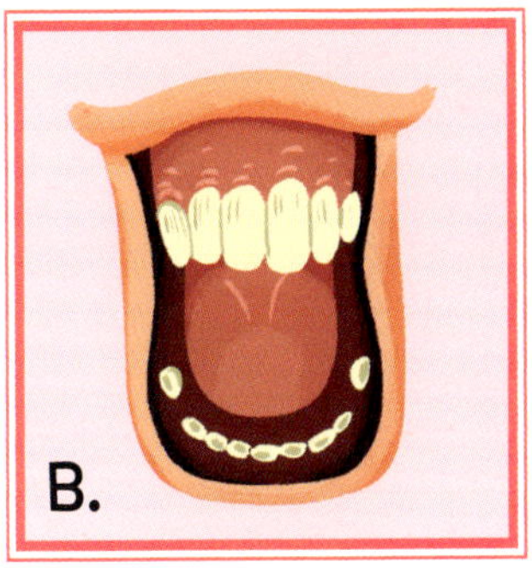

Dolphin

Hippopotamus

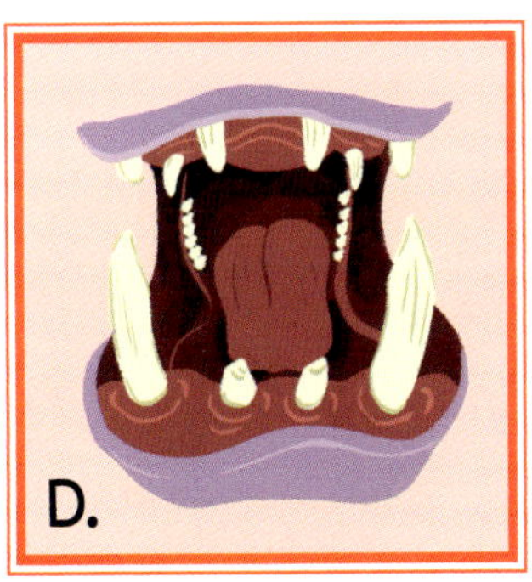

Horse

FOOD CHAINS

Q. Now I know about living things, what is a food chain?

A. Food chains are a way of showing how living things depend on each other for food. Food chains are made up of animals and plants. They are different in every habitat.

Plants are at the beginning of every food chain. Plants are followed by the herbivores that eat the plants. At the end, there are the omnivores or carnivores that eat the herbivores.

We can use a food chain to show that plants are eaten by squirrels, who are eaten by eagles.

PLANT

HERBIVORE

CARNIVORE

SAVANNA FOOD CHAIN

Q. What is a savanna?

A. Savannas are grassy plains with few trees.

This is a food chain from the savannas of Africa. Zebras eat grass and lions eat zebras.

Female lions catch most of the food for their pride (lions that live together in a group).

GRASS

ZEBRA

THINK ABOUT IT

Which animal is an herbivore in this food chain?

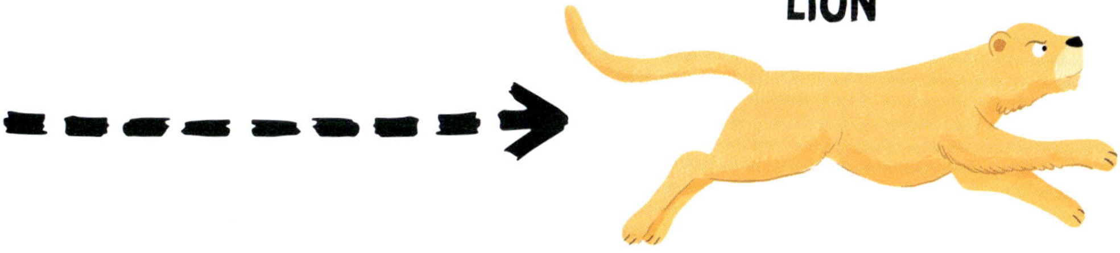

SEASHORE FOOD CHAIN

Q. Is the seashore the same as the sea?

A. A seashore is an area of land next to a sea or ocean.

Some plants and animals live away from the water on the sand or rocks. Other animals live in the water, close to the shore.

Rock pools are pools of seawater on the seashore. Small animals often live underwater in rock pools. They eat the shellfish and algae that live on the rocks.

FIND IT

Can you spot the plants and animals in the food chain below in the picture?

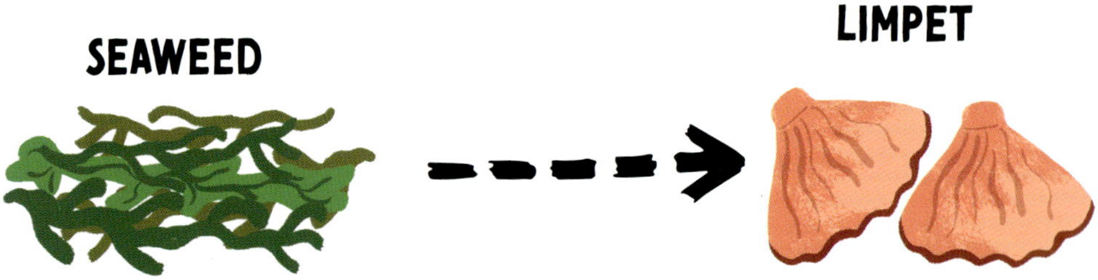

CRAB

OCEAN FOOD CHAIN

Q. Are there food chains in the ocean as well?

A. Yes! Lots of them.

Most of the Earth's surface is covered by oceans. Fish, shellfish, and ocean mammals spend most of their lives underwater. Plants, such as seaweed and algae, grow on the ocean floor.

Many predators, such as large fish and sharks, live in the ocean. These predators eat smaller fish that feed on algae.

THINK ABOUT IT

Here is a food chain drawn in a special way. What is in the food chain? Which animal is both a predator and prey?

Can you draw a food chain like this?

WOODLAND FOOD CHAIN

Q. There are woods near my house. Will there be any food chains there?

A. Yes! Even small habitats have many food chains.

Woodlands are home to many types of animal, including large mammals, birds, and tiny insects. It can be hard to spot insects because they live in logs and under fallen leaves.

There is plenty of food for herbivores in woodland habitats. Herbivores, such as deer, eat the leaves and fruits of small plants and trees. Woodland carnivores, such as wolves, eat the herbivores.

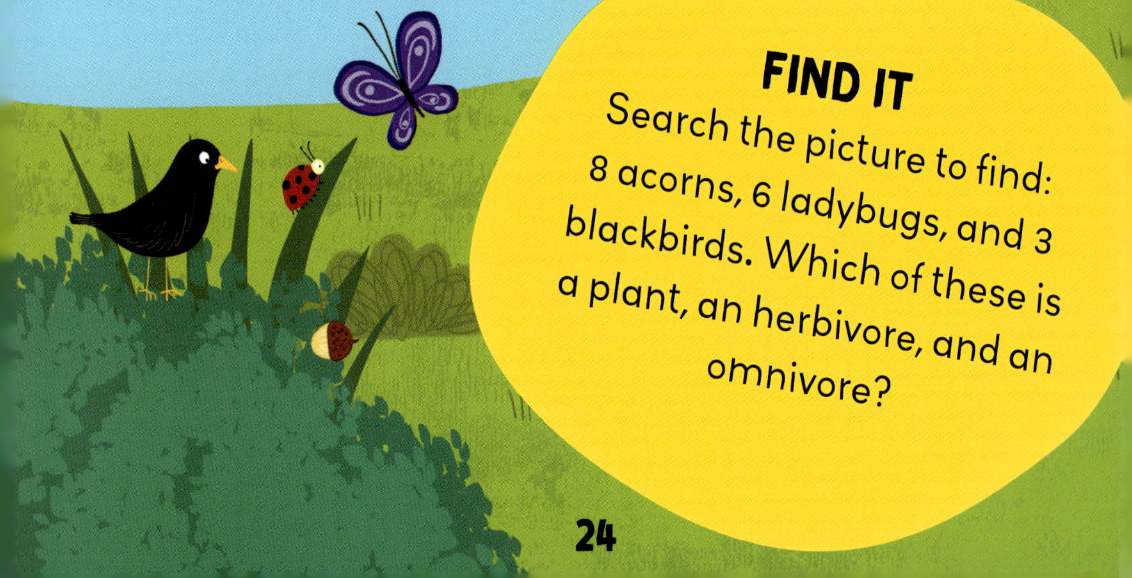

FIND IT

Search the picture to find: 8 acorns, 6 ladybugs, and 3 blackbirds. Which of these is a plant, an herbivore, and an omnivore?

RAINFOREST FOOD CHAIN

Q. Why are rainforests so special?

A. There are many reasons, but one reason is that they are full of animals that don't live anywhere else.

There are lots of food chains in rainforests. Many tall trees grow up from the forest floor. On the forest floor are leaves and plants and lots of types of insect and other animals. Most large animals live close to the ground, as they are too heavy to climb up into the trees.

Small birds and monkeys often live high in the branches of rainforest trees. They eat the fruits and leaves of rainforest plants.

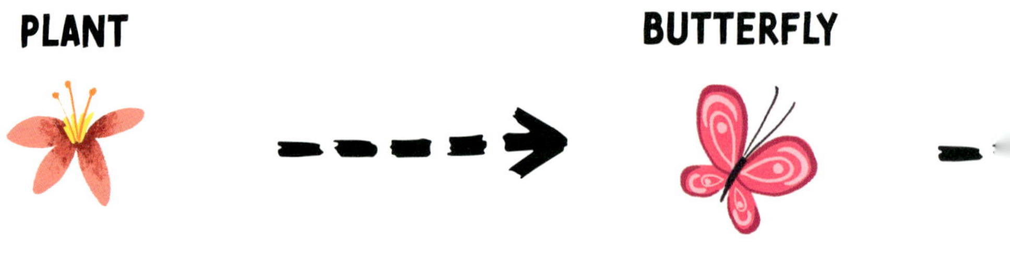

FIND IT

Can you find the animals in the food chain below in the picture?

TOUCAN

JAGUAR

HUMANS

Q. Am I a part of a food chain?

A. Yes. Humans are part of food chains too.

Humans are part of food chains because all of our food comes from plants and animals. Humans are usually at the end of food chains.

Humans grow plants and raise animals on farms. On a farm, a farmer grows grass for sheep to eat. Then, some humans eat meat from the sheep.

THINK ABOUT IT

How many food chains can you see in this picture?

QUIZ

1. Plants aren't living things. True or not true?

a) true

b) not true

2. What is the name for an animal that only eats other animals?

a) herbivore

b) omnivore

c) carnivore

3. Tigers are predators. True or not true?

a) true

b) not true

4. What comes at the beginning of a food chain?

a) herbivores

b) plants

c) carnivores

5. Which of these plants grows in the ocean?

a) seaweed

b) oak tree

c) daisy

6. Humans grow most of the plants that they eat. True or not true?

a) true

b) not true

Quiz answers

1. b – not true (plants and animals are living things)
2. c – carnivore
3. a – true
4. b – plants
5. a – seaweed
6. a – true

GLOSSARY

algae a plant-like living thing without a stem or leaves

carnivore an animal that only eats meat

claw a sharp curved nail on the foot of an animal

female describes an animal that can give birth to young or lay eggs from which young will hatch

food chain a way of showing how living things depend on each other for food

habitat the area where plants and animals live

herbivore an animal that only eats plants

mammal a type of animal with fur that gives birth to live young

omnivore an animal that eats plants and meat. "Omni" means all

predator an animal that kills and eats other animals

prey an animal that is killed and eaten by other animals

raise to look after an animal or plant as it grows

rock pool a pool of seawater on a rocky beach

savanna a flat area of land covered in grass and some trees

scavenger an animal that feeds on the bodies of other dead animals

surface the top part of something

survive to stay alive and not die

INDEX

SOME ANSWERS

p. 6 water lilies – pond; cactus – desert; seaweed – ocean; rose – garden
p. 10 there are 10
p. 12. carnivores: A, D, E, H; omnivores: B, C, F, G
p. 14. A – dolphin; B – horse; C – tiger; D – hippopotamus
p. 18. zebra
p. 22. seal
p. 24 acorns are plants; ladybugs and blackbirds are omnivores and may be eaten by carnivores or other omnivores